P9-CRB-292

Name

Date

To parents
Have your child write his or her name in the box above. On this page, your child will connect the first three uppercase letters of the alphabet. From this page on, the number of letters will gradually increase. Please have your child say the letters aloud while he or she is tracing.

■ While saying each letter aloud, draw a line from "A" to "C" to connect the letters in alphabetical order.

Writing "A·B·C"

■ Say the name of each letter. Then say the sound of the letter as you trace it. Follow the stroke order indicated by the numbers.

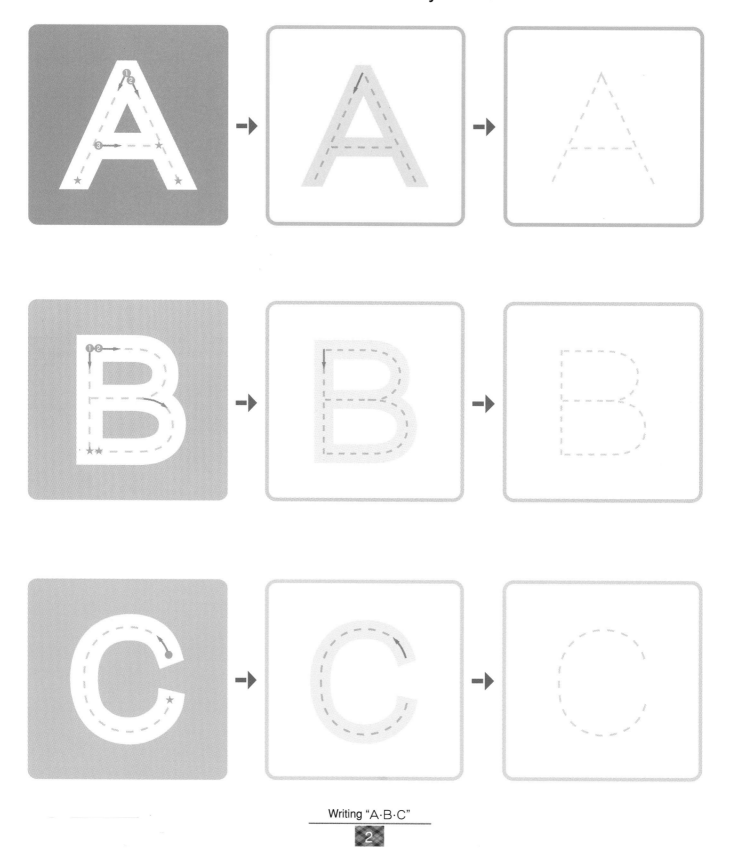

Uppercase Letters
Saying "A→F"

■ While saying each letter aloud, draw a line from "A" to "F" to connect the letters in alphabetical order.

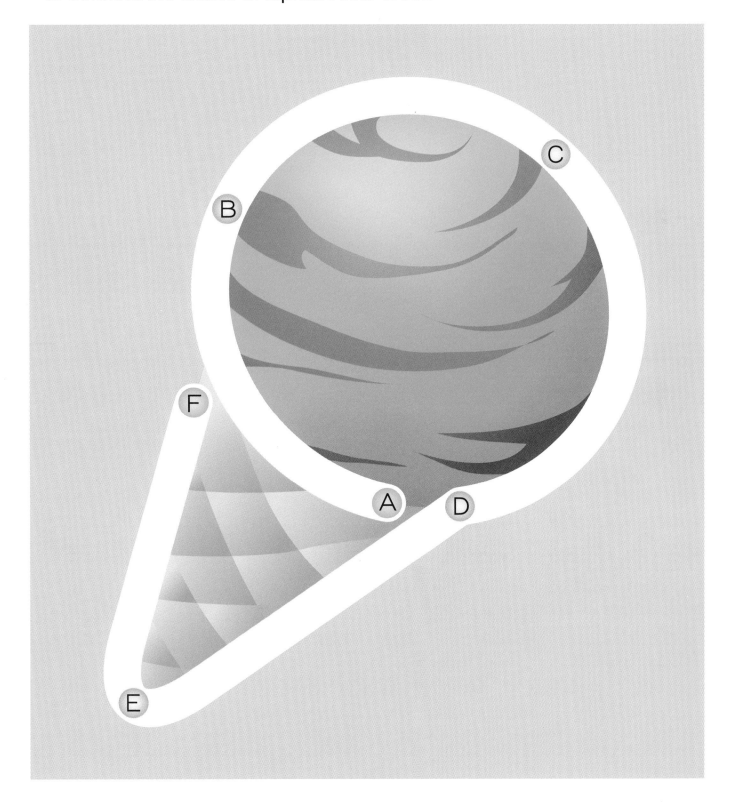

Writing "D·E·F"

■ Say the name of each letter. Then say the sound of the letter as you trace it. Follow the stroke order indicated by the numbers.

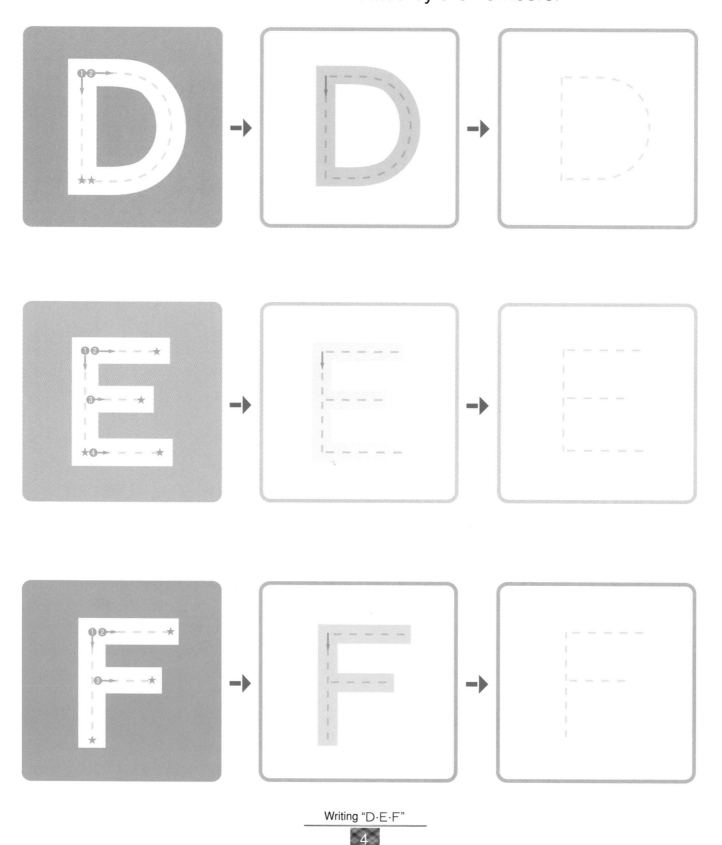

Uppercase Letters
Saying "A→I"

Name

Date

■ While saying each letter aloud, draw a line from "A" to "I" to connect the letters in alphabetical order.

Writing "G·H·I"

■ Say the name of each letter. Then say the sound of the letter as you trace it. Follow the stroke order indicated by the numbers.

Uppercase Letters
Saying "A→L"

■ While saying each letter aloud, draw a line from "A" to "L" to connect the letters in alphabetical order.

Writing "J·K·L"

■ Say the name of each letter. Then say the sound of the letter as you trace it. Follow the stroke order indicated by the numbers.

Uppercase Letters
Saying "A→O"

Name

Date

■ While saying each letter aloud, draw a line from "A" to "O" to connect the letters in alphabetical order.

Writing "M·N·O"

■ Say the name of each letter. Then say the sound of the letter as you trace it. Follow the stroke order indicated by the numbers.

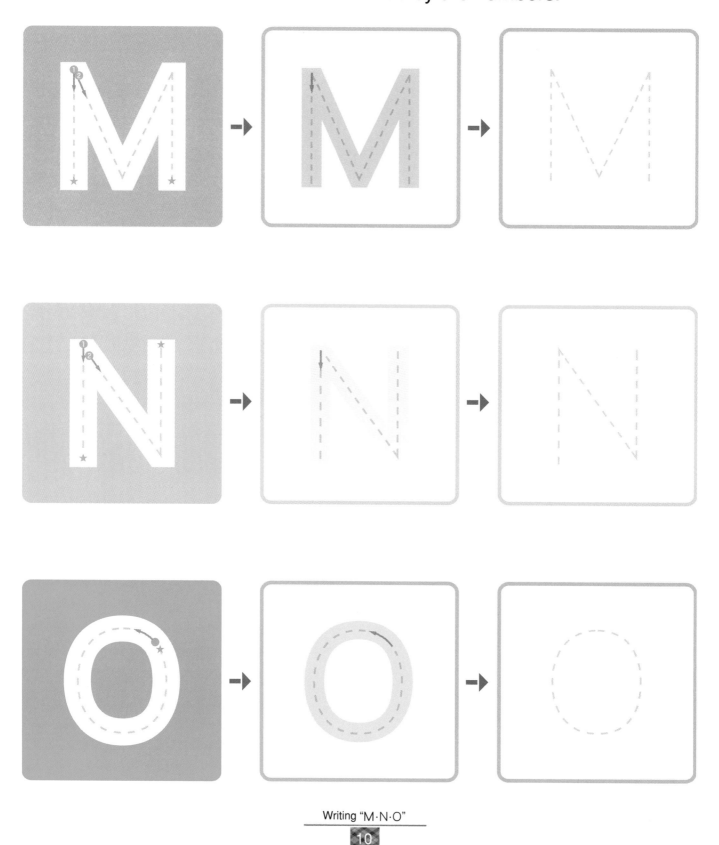

Uppercase Letters
Saying "A→R"

■ While saying each letter aloud, draw a line from "A" to "R" to connect the letters in alphabetical order.

Writing "P·Q·R"

■ Say the name of each letter. Then say the sound of the letter as you trace it. Follow the stroke order indicated by the numbers.

Uppercase Letters
Saying "A→U"

Name

Date

■ While saying each letter aloud, draw a line from "A" to "U" to connect the letters in alphabetical order.

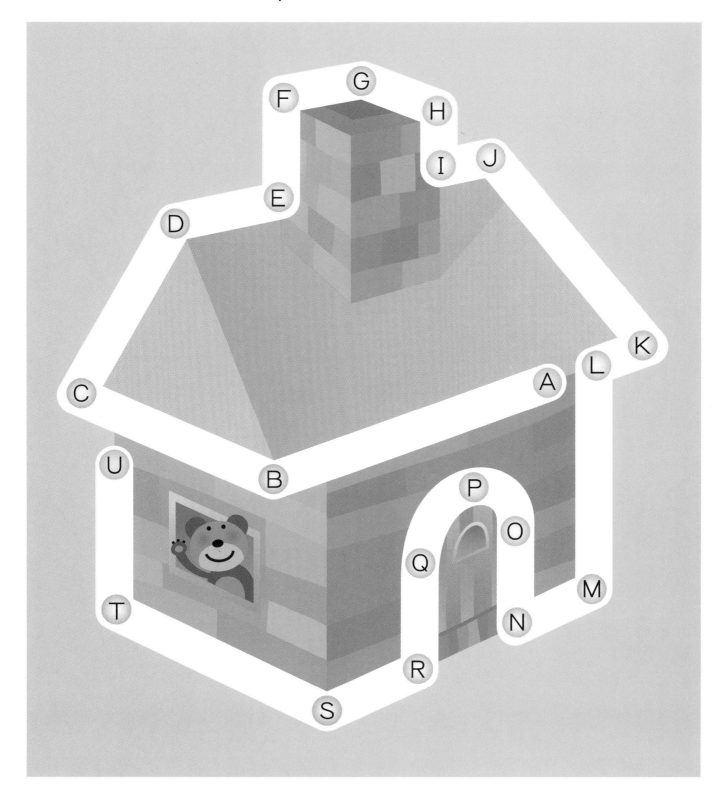

Writing "S·T·U"

■ Say the name of each letter. Then say the sound of the letter as you trace it. Follow the stroke order indicated by the numbers.

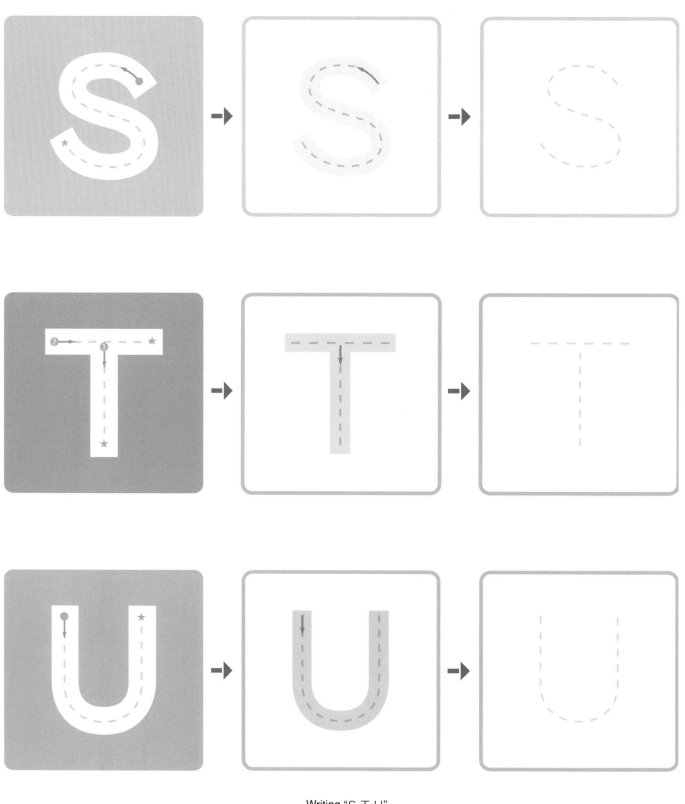

8 **Uppercase Letters**
Saying "A→X"

Name

Date

■ While saying each letter aloud, draw a line from "A" to "X" to connect the letters in alphabetical order.

J   L
K
H   I   M   N
G   O
F   Q
E   R   P   U
C   A   T
D   S   V
B   W
X

Writing "V·W·X"

■ Say the name of each letter. Then say the sound of the letter as you trace it. Follow the stroke order indicated by the numbers.

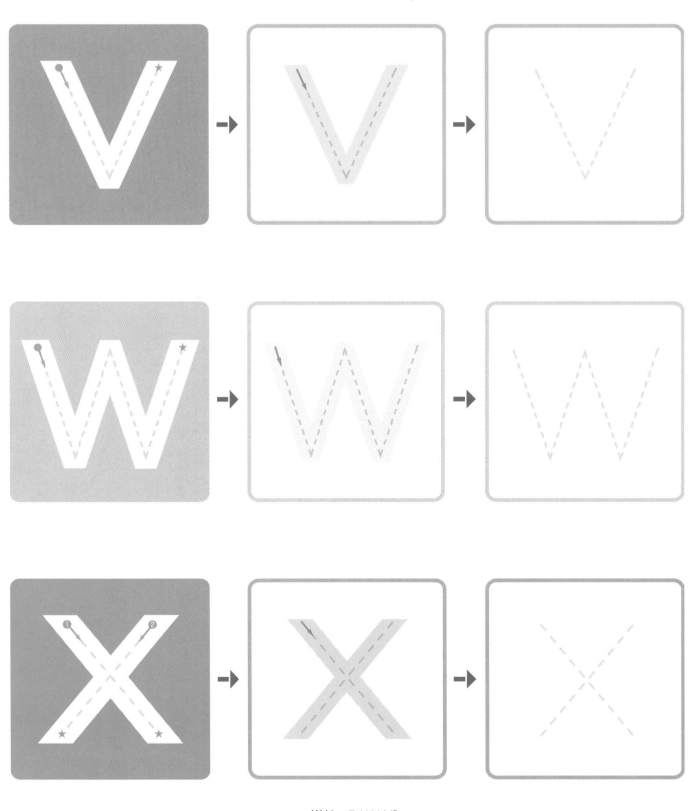

Uppercase Letters
Saying "A→Z"

■ While saying each letter aloud, draw a line from "A" to "Z" to connect the letters in alphabetical order.

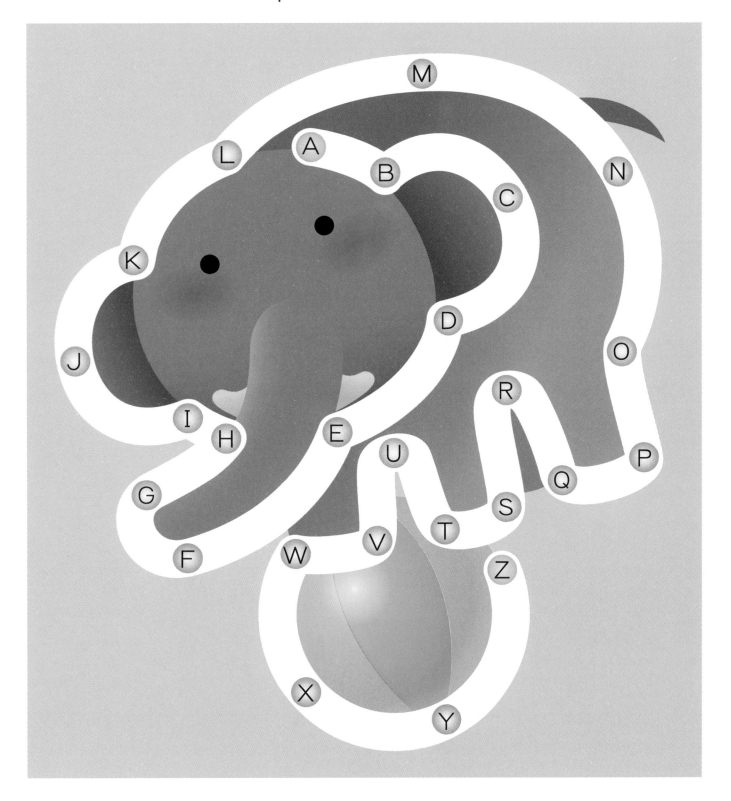

Writing "Y·Z"

■ Say the name of each letter. Then say the sound of the letter as you trace it. Follow the stroke order indicated by the numbers.

Lowercase Letters
Saying "a·b·c"

Name
Date

To parents
On this page, your child will connect the first three lowercase letters of the alphabet. From this page on, the number of letters will gradually increase. Please have your child say the letters aloud while he or she is connecting the dots. The answer to each puzzle can be found at the bottom of the following page.

■ While saying each letter aloud, draw a line from "a" to "c" to connect the letters in alphabetical order.

Writing "a·b·c"

■ Say the name of each letter. Then say the sound of the letter as you trace it. Follow the stroke order indicated by the numbers.

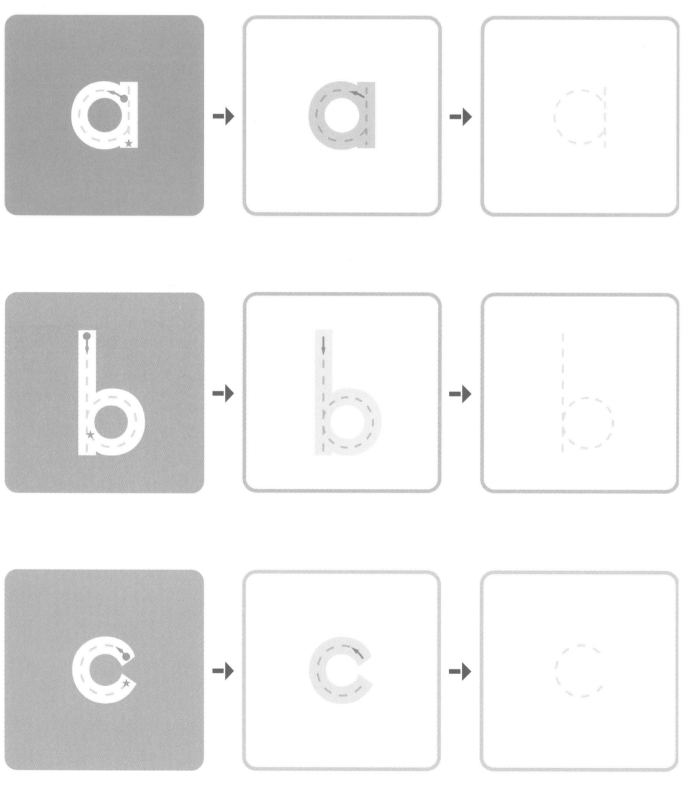

(P19 Answer - fish)

Lowercase Letters
Saying "a → f"

Name	
Date	

■ While saying each letter aloud, draw a line from "a" to "f"
to connect the letters in alphabetical order.

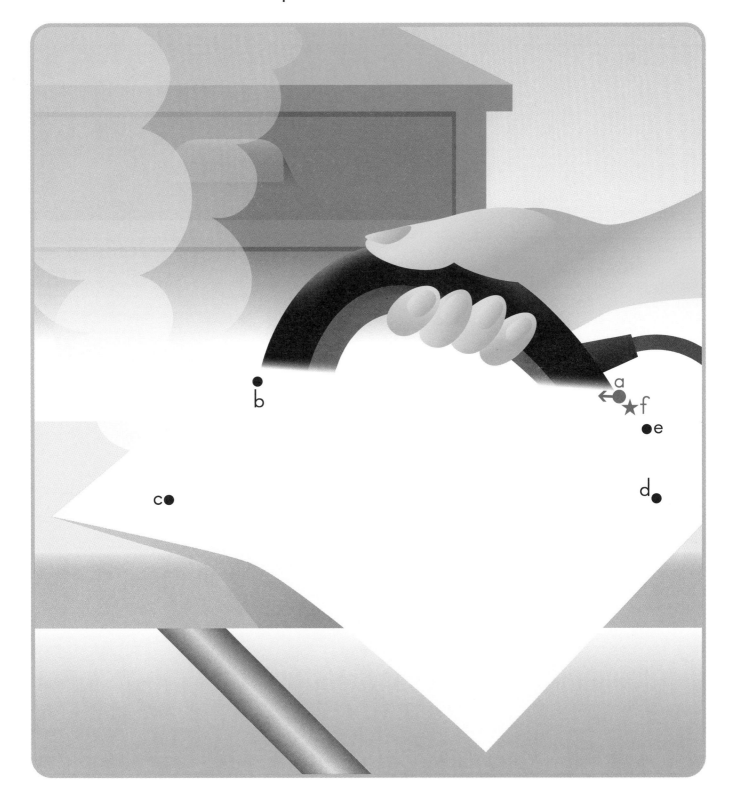

Writing "d.e.f"

■ Say the name of each letter. Then say the sound of the letter as you trace it. Follow the stroke order indicated by the numbers.

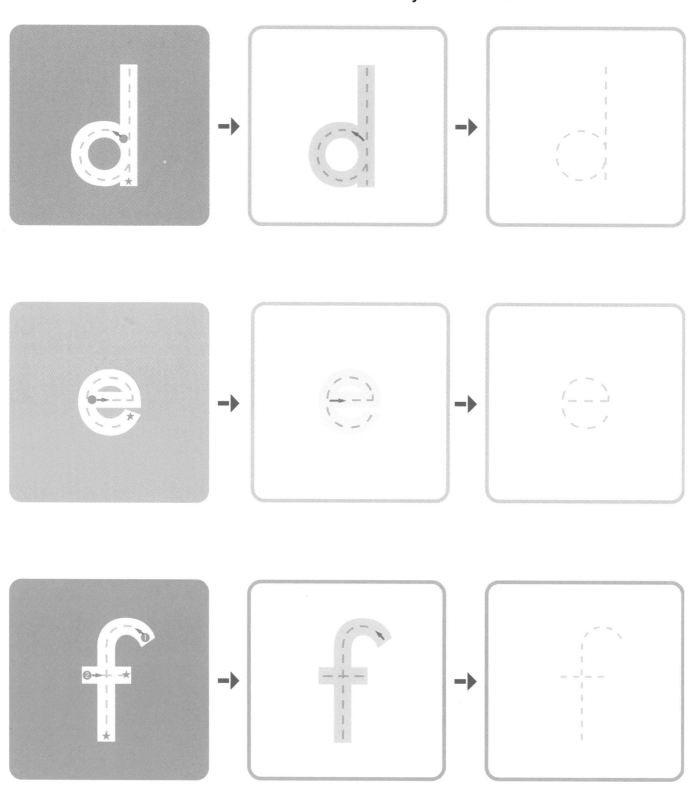

(P21 Answer - iron)

Lowercase Letters
Saying "a → i"

■ While saying each letter aloud, draw a line from "a" to "i" to connect the letters in alphabetical order.

Writing "g·h·i"

■ Say the name of each letter. Then say the sound of the letter as you trace it. Follow the stroke order indicated by the numbers.

(P23 Answer - frying pan)

Lowercase Letters
Saying "a → l"

■ While saying each letter aloud, draw a line from "a" to "l" to connect the letters in alphabetical order.

j i h

k● g●

a

★l
c b

●d

e f

Writing "j·k·l"

■ Say the name of each letter. Then say the sound of the letter as you trace it. Follow the stroke order indicated by the numbers.

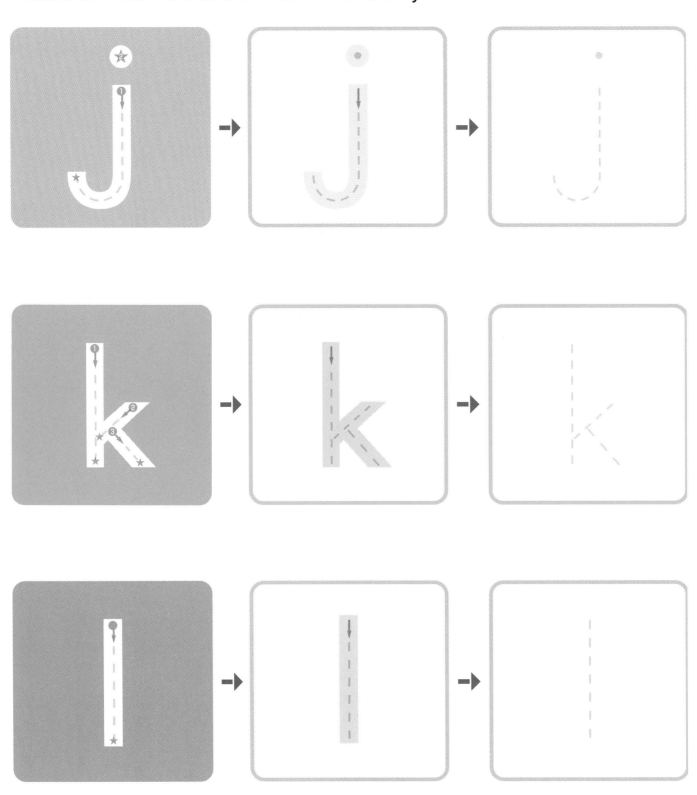

(P25 Answer - cap)

Lowercase Letters
Saying "a → o"

Name

Date

■ While saying each letter aloud, draw a line from "a" to "o" to connect the letters in alphabetical order.

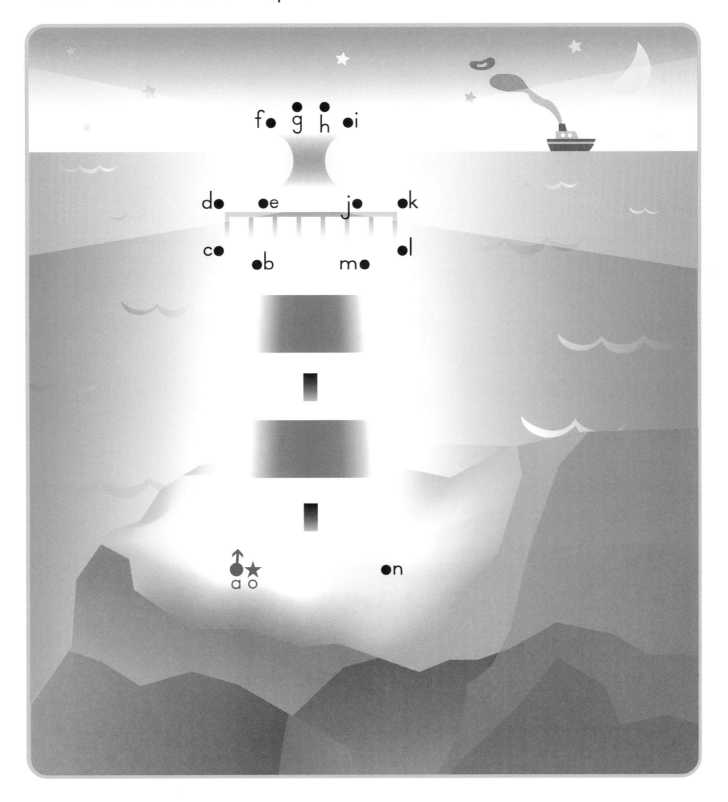

Writing "m·n·o"

■ Say the name of each letter. Then say the sound of the letter as you trace it. Follow the stroke order indicated by the numbers.

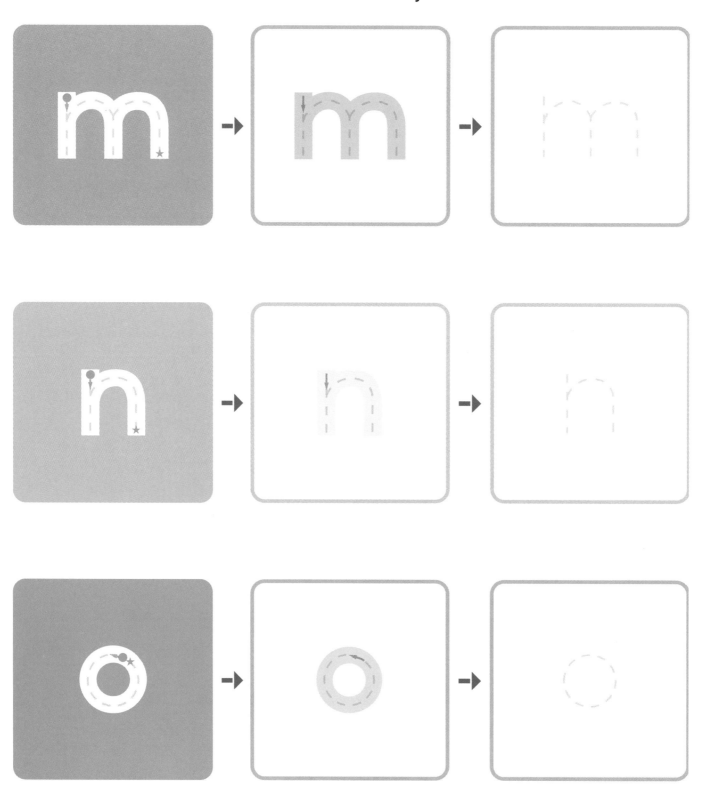

(P27 Answer - lighthouse)

Lowercase Letters
Saying "a → r"

Name

Date

■ While saying each letter aloud, draw a line from "a" to "r" to connect the letters in alphabetical order.

Writing "p·q·r"

■ Say the name of each letter. Then say the sound of the letter as you trace it. Follow the stroke order indicated by the numbers.

Lowercase Letters
Saying "a → u"

Name

Date

■ While saying each letter aloud, draw a line from "a" to "u" to connect the letters in alphabetical order.

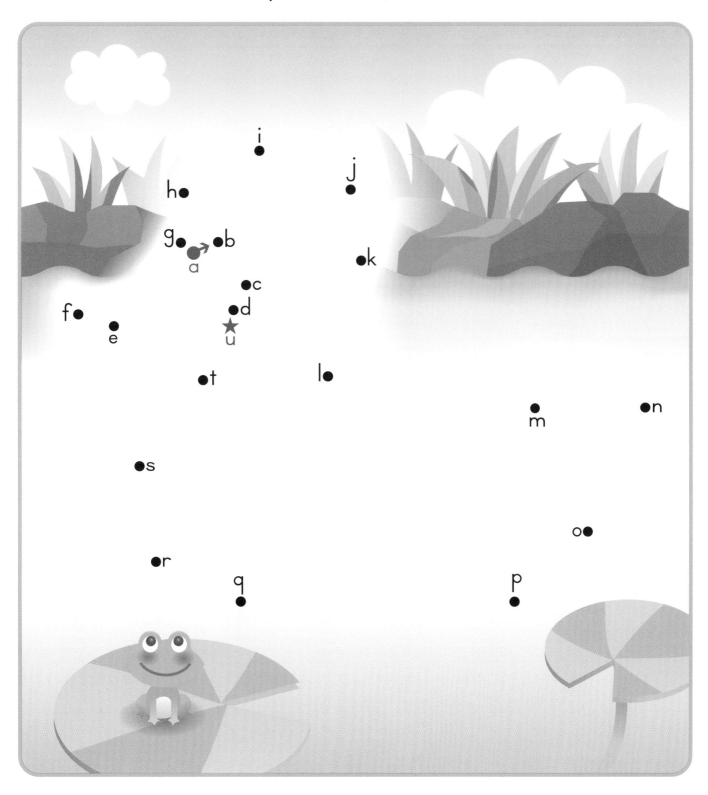

Writing "s·t·u"

■ Say the name of each letter. Then say the sound of the letter as you trace it. Follow the stroke order indicated by the numbers.

(P31 Answer - duck)

Lowercase Letters
Saying "a → x"

■ While saying each letter aloud, draw a line from "a" to "x" to connect the letters in alphabetical order.

l

n

j

k

m

i

o

u

d

h

g q

p

e

t

v

c

s

b

w

f   r

a x

Writing "v·w·x"

■ Say the name of each letter. Then say the sound of the letter as you trace it. Follow the stroke order indicated by the numbers.

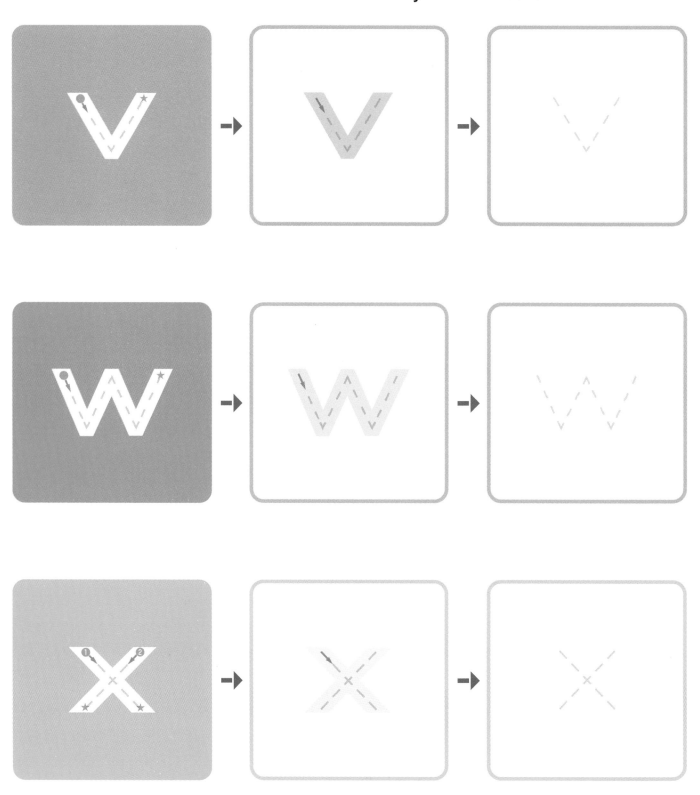

Lowercase Letters

Saying "a → z"

■ While saying each letter aloud, draw a line from "a" to "z"
  to connect the letters in alphabetical order.

Writing "y·z"

■ Say the name of each letter. Then say the sound of the letter as you trace it. Follow the stroke order indicated by the numbers.

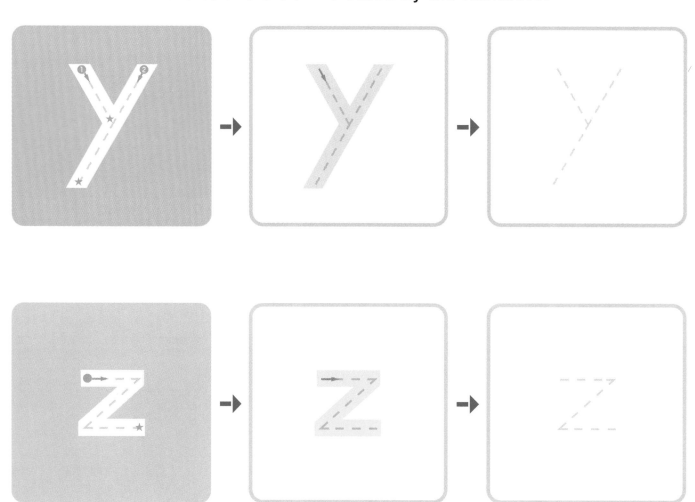

(P35 Answer - bulldog)

Name

Date

■ Trace the letters "A" to "Z" while saying each letter aloud.

A   B   C   D

E   F   G   H

I   J   K   L

M   N   O   P

Q   R   S   T

U   V   W   X

Y   Z

Writing "a → z"

■ Trace the letters "a" to "z" while saying each letter aloud.

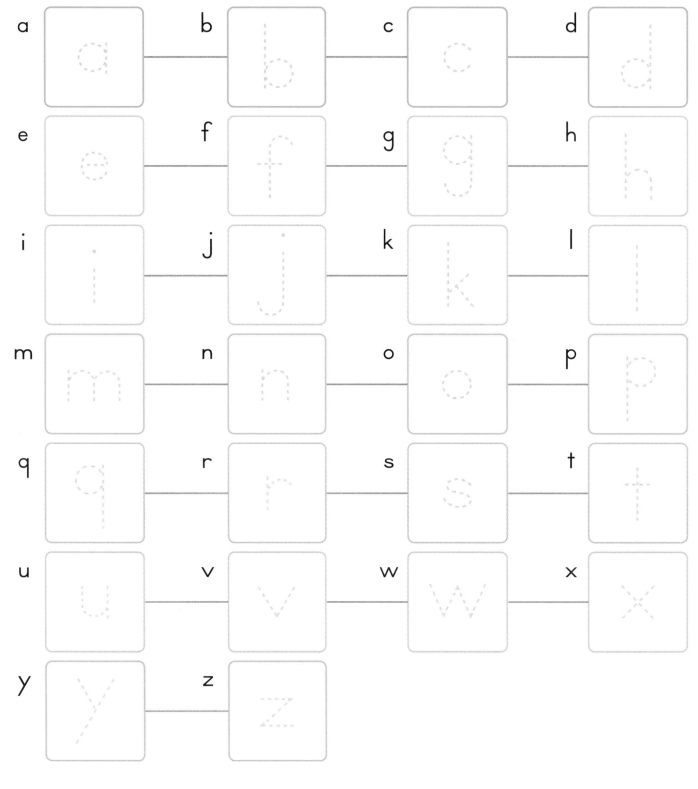

Upper- and Lower-case Letters
Writing "A·a / B·b"

Name

Date

To parents
In this exercise, your child will practice linking uppercase letters to their lowercase counterparts. Please help your child read the names of the characters. Then point out that each pair of words start with the same letter—one uppercase and one lowercase.

■ Look at the first letters of the words below. Then trace the letters.

Writing "A·a / B·b"

■ Trace and then write each letter while saying it aloud.

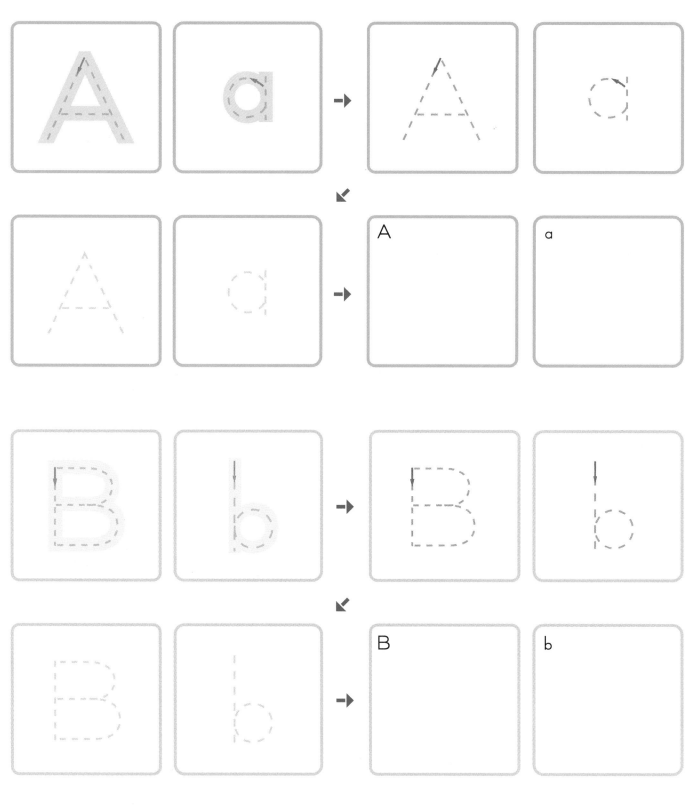

Upper- and Lower-case Letters
Writing "C·c / D·d"

■ Look at the first letters of the words below. Then trace the letters.

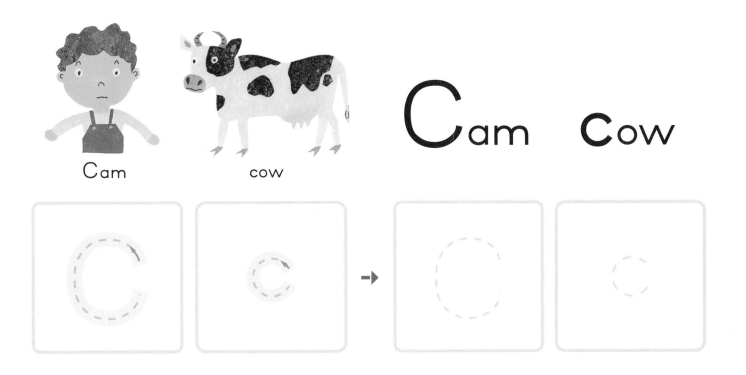

Cam   cow

Cam   Cow

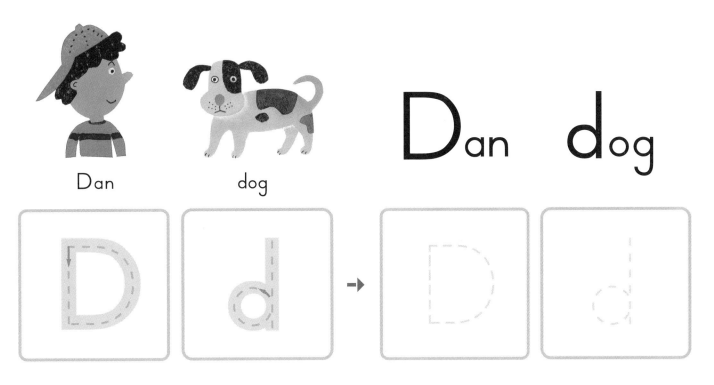

Dan   dog

Dan   dog

Writing "C·c / D·d"

■ Trace and then write each letter while saying it aloud.

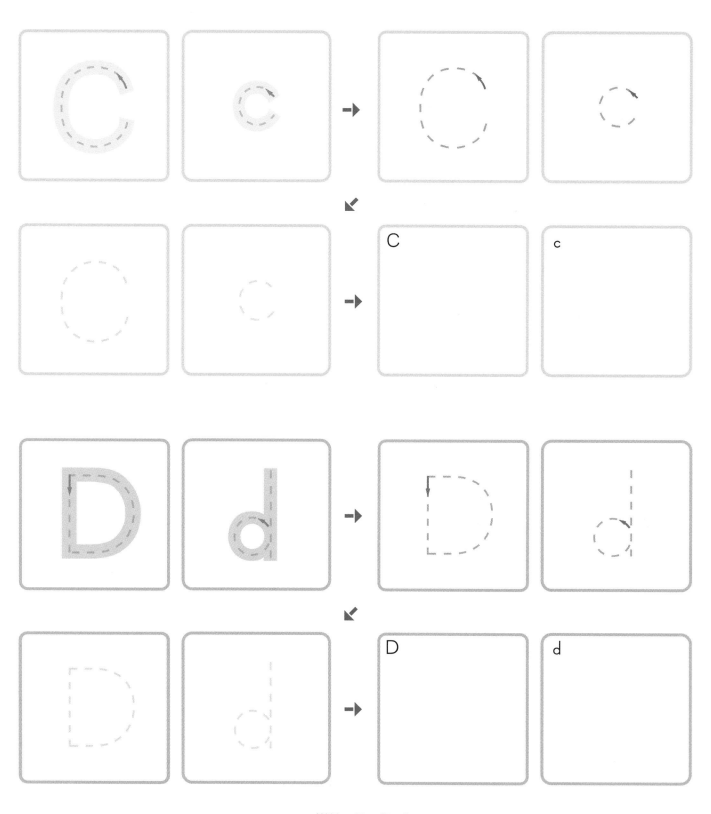

22 Review
Writing "A·a→ D·d"

■ Trace each letter while saying it aloud.

Writing "A·a → D·d"

■ Trace and then write each letter while saying it aloud.

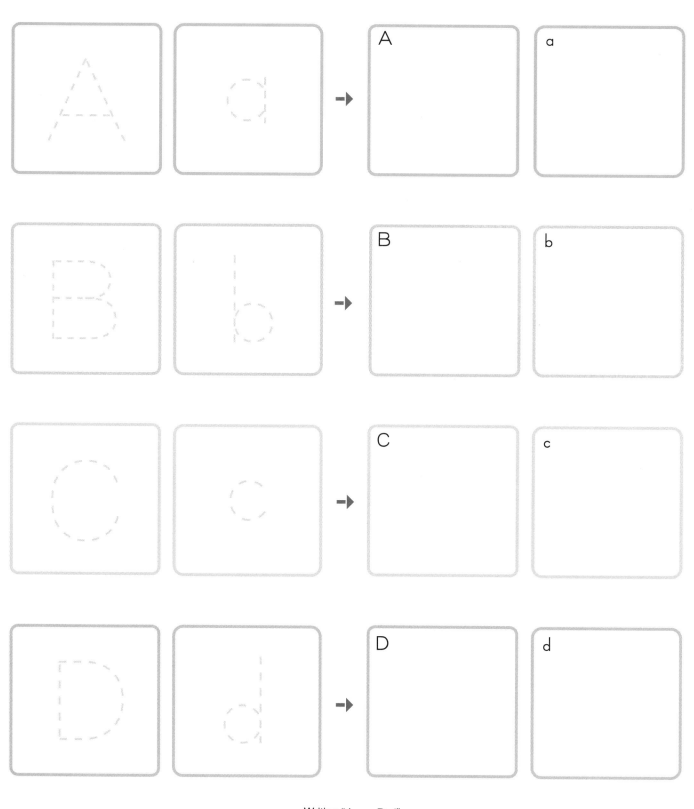

Upper- and Lower-case Letters

Writing "E·e / F·f"

Name

Date

■ Look at the first letters of the words below. Then trace the letters.

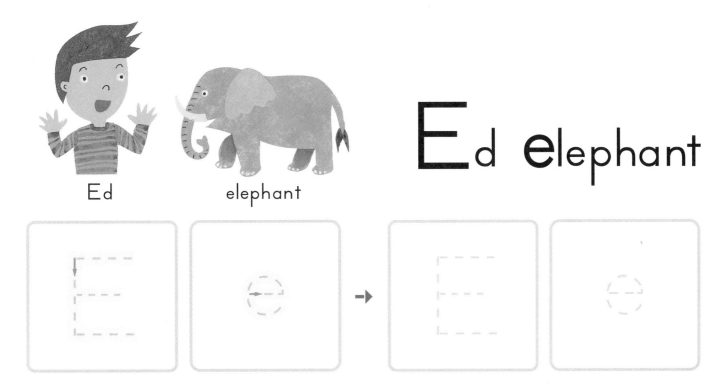

Ed   elephant

E_d elephant

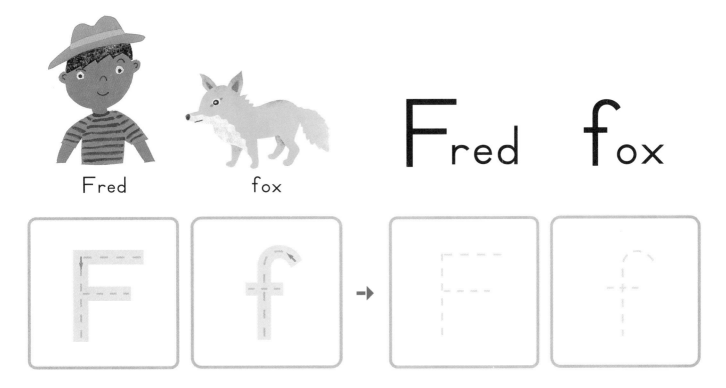

Fred   fox

F_{red}   f_{ox}

Writing "E·e / F·f"

■ Trace and then write each letter while saying it aloud.

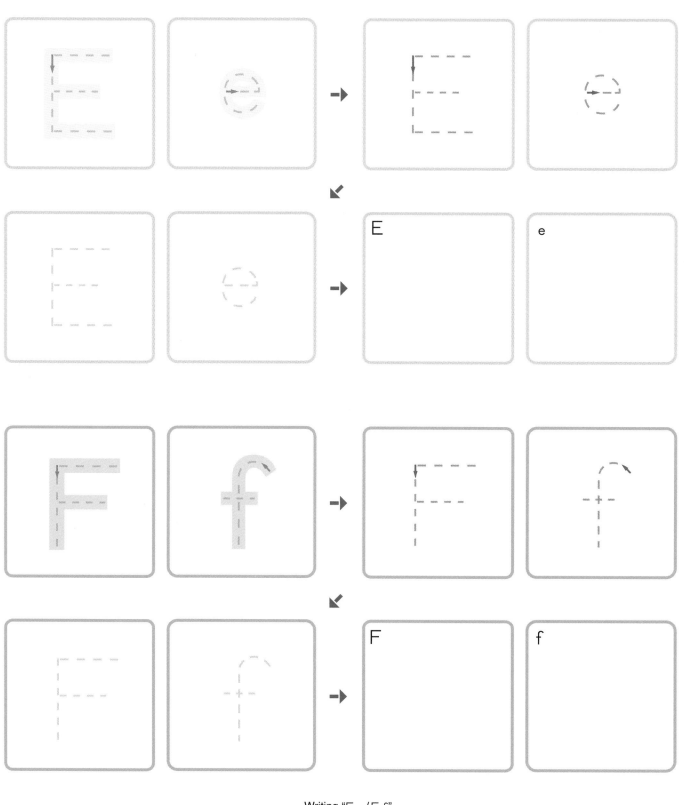

24 Upper- and Lower-case Letters
Writing "G·g/H·h"

Name

Date

■ Look at the first letters of the words below. Then trace the letters.

Gus   goat

Gus   **g**oat

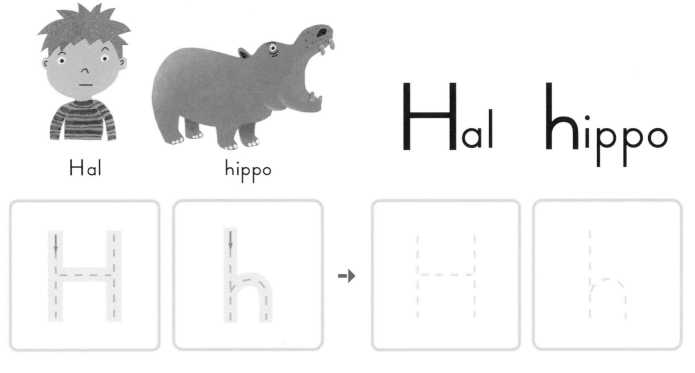

Hal   hippo

Hal   **h**ippo

Writing "G·g/H·h"

47

Writing "G.g/H.h"

■ Trace and then write each letter while saying it aloud.

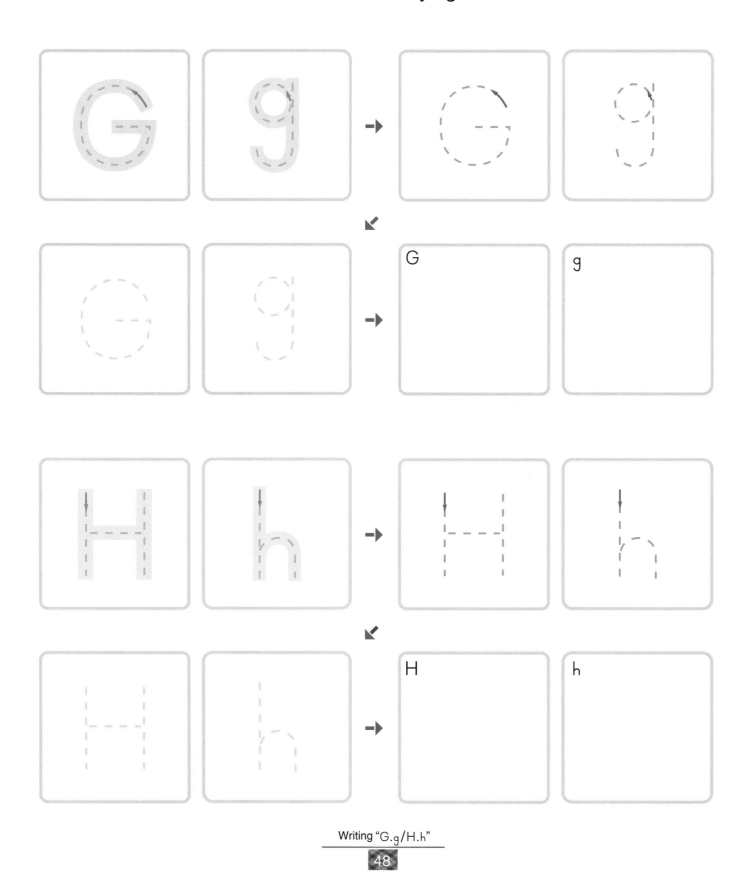

25 **Review**
Writing "E·e → H·h"

Name
Date

■ Trace each letter while saying it aloud.

  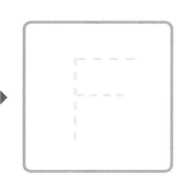 

  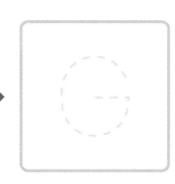 

Writing "E·e→H·h"

■ Trace and then write each letter while saying it aloud.

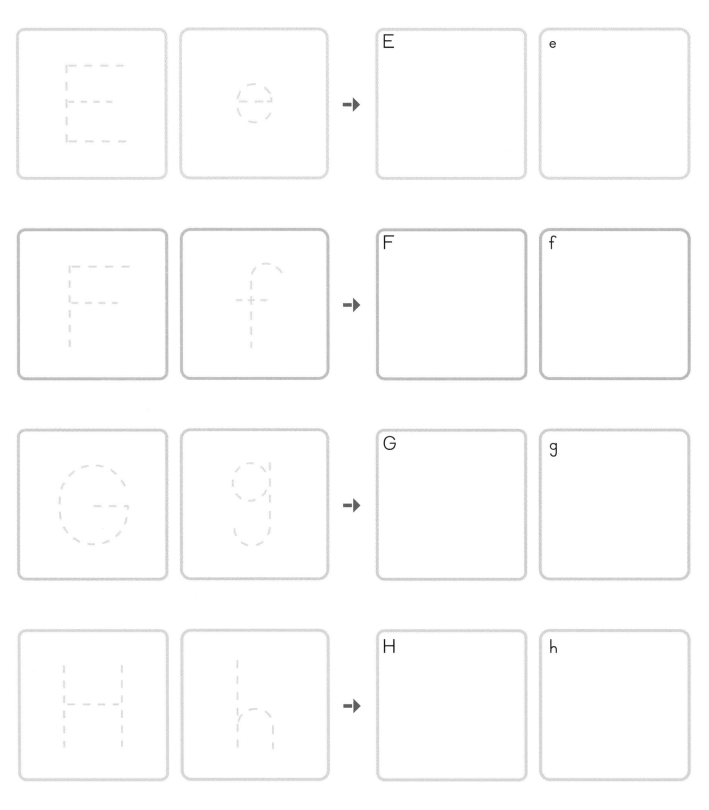

Upper- and Lower-case Letters
Writing "I·i / J·j"

Name

Date

■ Look at the first letters of the words below. Then trace the letters.

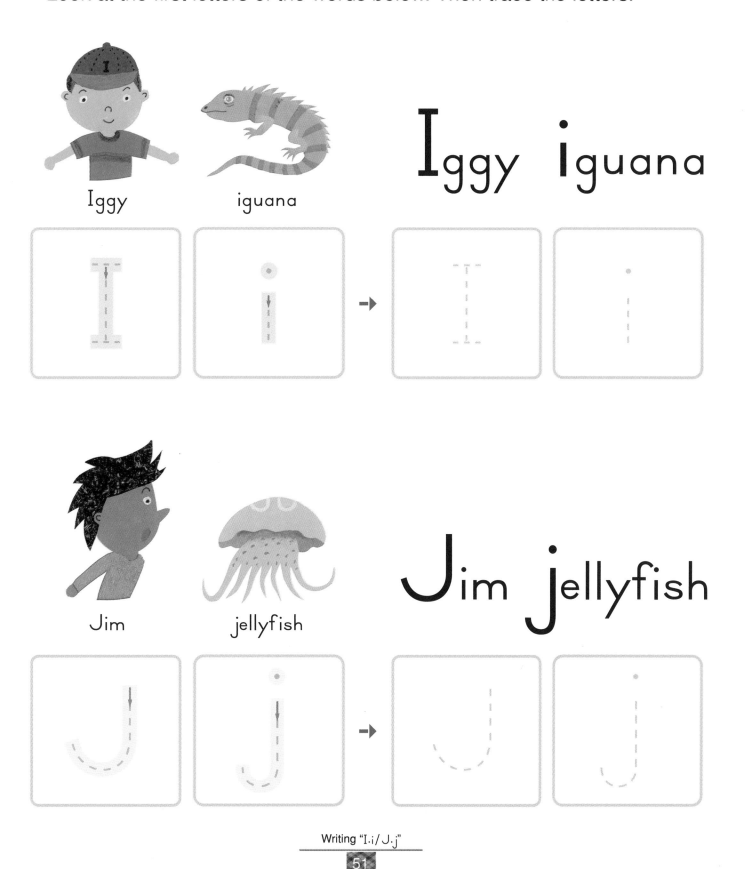

Iggy   iguana

Iggy iguana

Jim   jellyfish

Jim jellyfish

Writing "I·i / J·j"

■ Trace and then write each letter while saying it aloud.

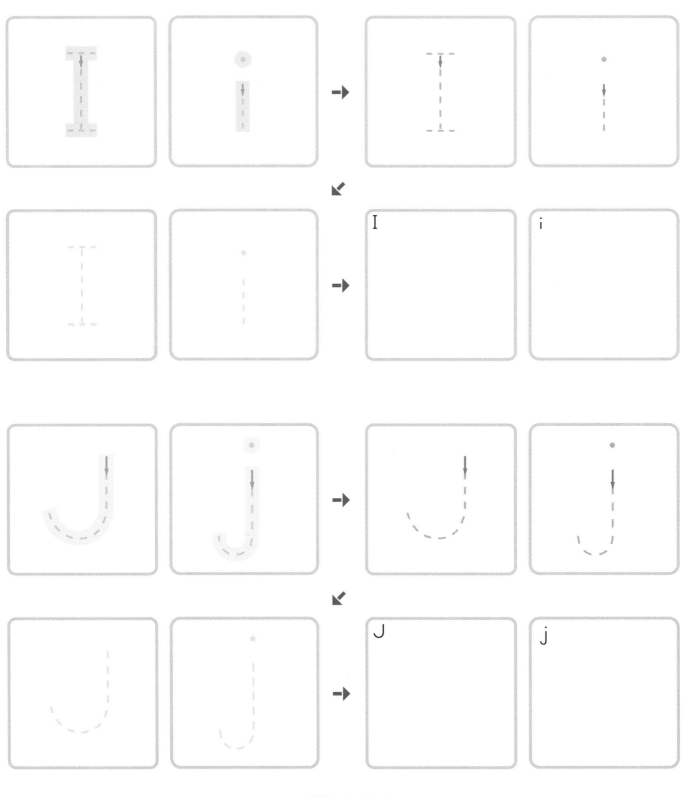

Upper- and Lower-case Letters
Writing "K·k / L·l"

Name

Date

■ Look at the first letters of the words below. Then trace the letters.

Kim   kitten

Kim   kitten

K   k   →   K   k

Larry   lion

Larry   lion

L   l   →   L   l

Writing "K·k/L·l"

■ Trace and then write each letter while saying it aloud.

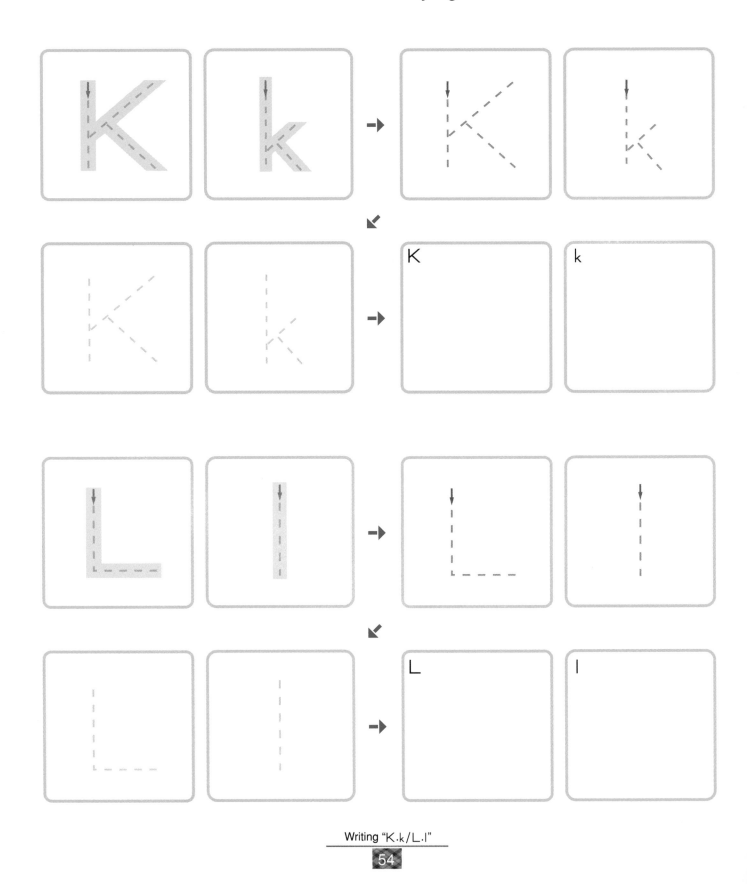

Name

Date

■ Trace each letter while saying it aloud.

I	i	→	I	i
J	j	→	J	j
K	k	→	K	k
L	l	→	L	l

Writing "I·i → L·l"

■ Trace and then write each letter while saying it aloud.

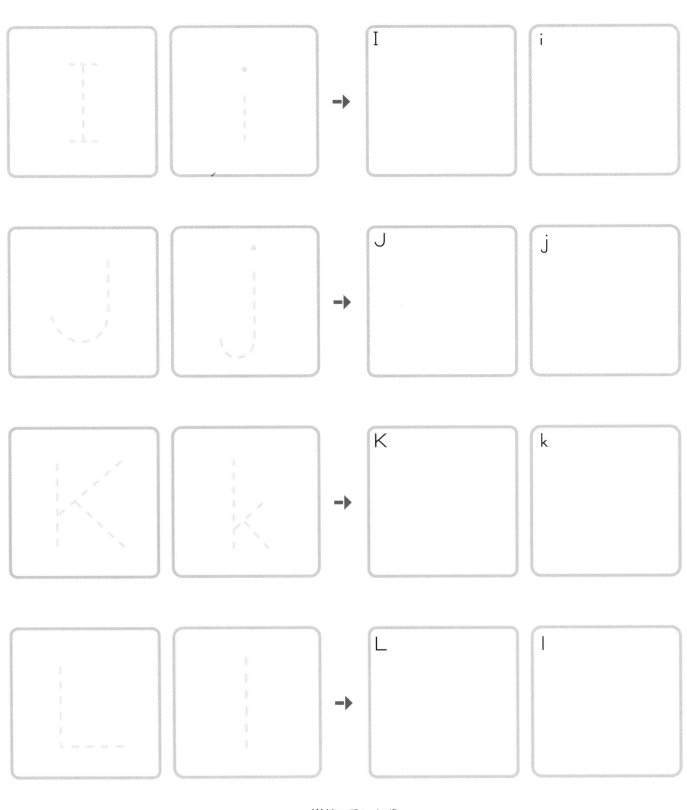

Upper- and Lower-case Letters
Writing "M·m / N·n"

Name

Date

■ Look at the first letters of the words below. Then trace the letters.

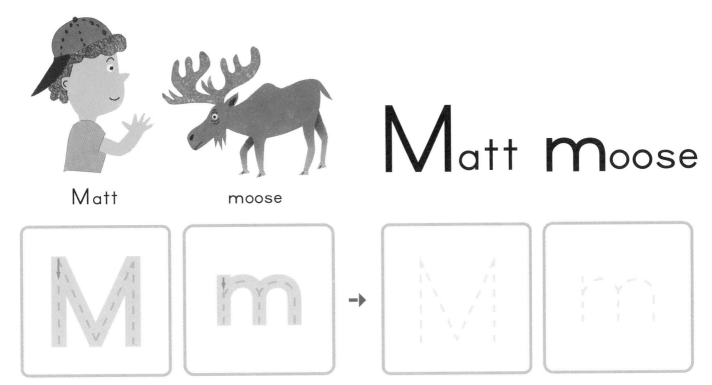

Matt   moose

Matt moose

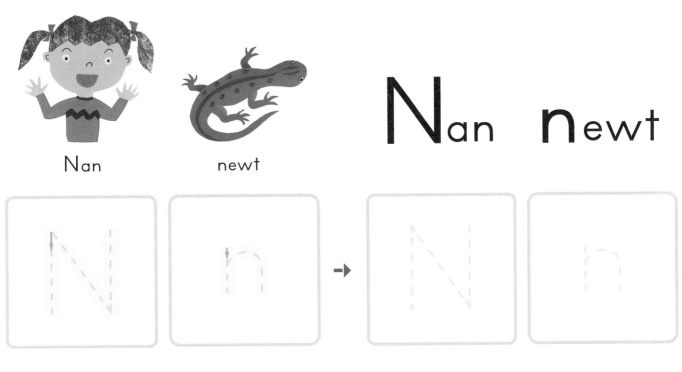

Nan   newt

Nan newt

Writing "M·m / N·n"

■ Trace and then write each letter while saying it aloud.

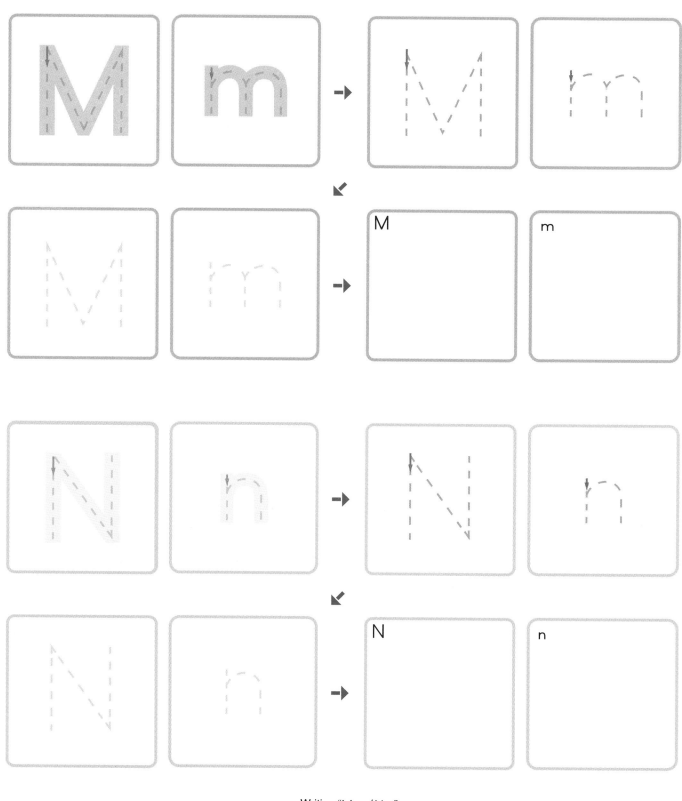

Name

Date

■ Look at the first letters of the words below. Then trace the letters.

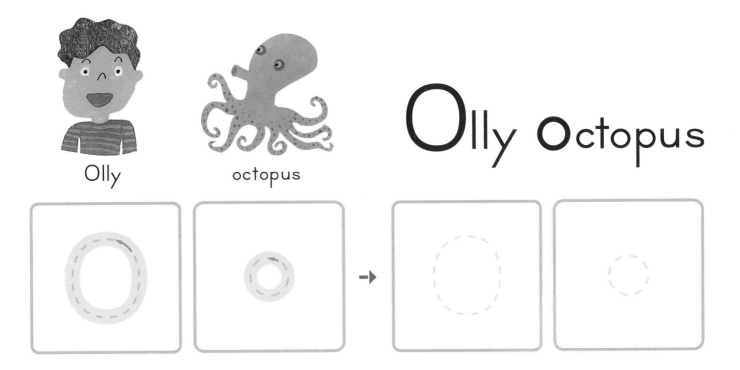

Olly   octopus   Olly Octopus

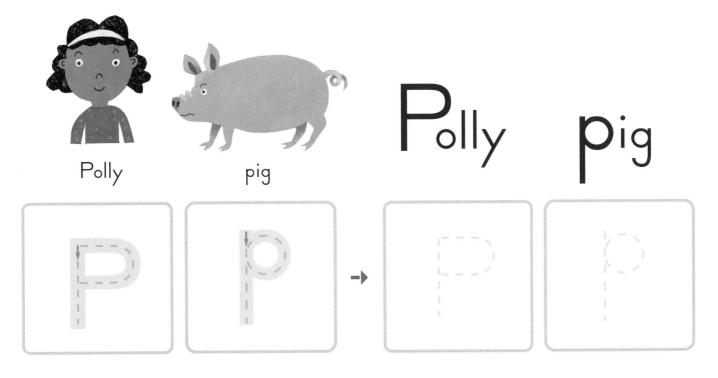

Polly   pig   Polly pig

Writing "O·o / P·p"

■ Trace and then write each letter while saying it aloud.

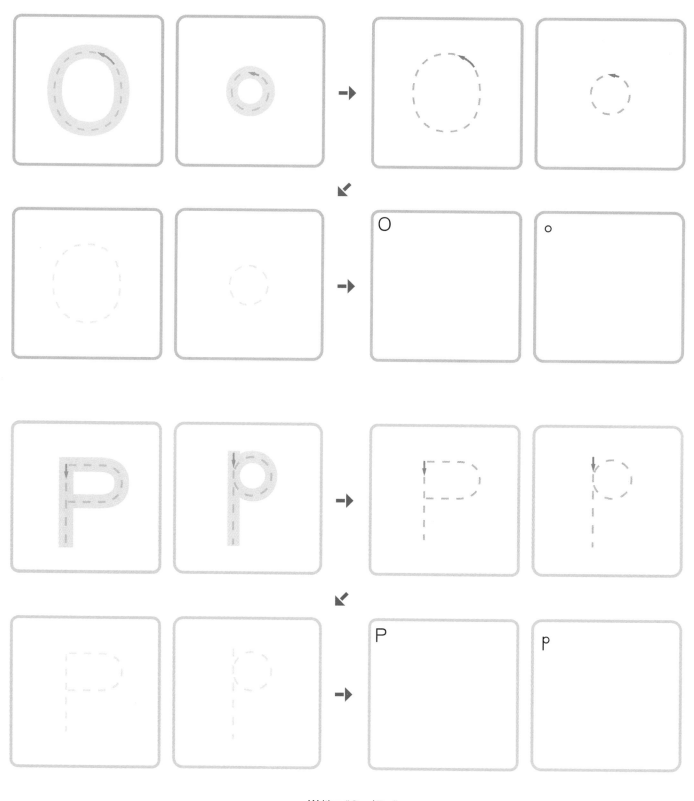

Review
Writing "M·m → P·p"

■ Trace each letter while saying it aloud.

M m → M m

N n → N n

O o → O o

P p → P p

Writing "M·m → P·p"

■ Trace and then write each letter while saying it aloud.

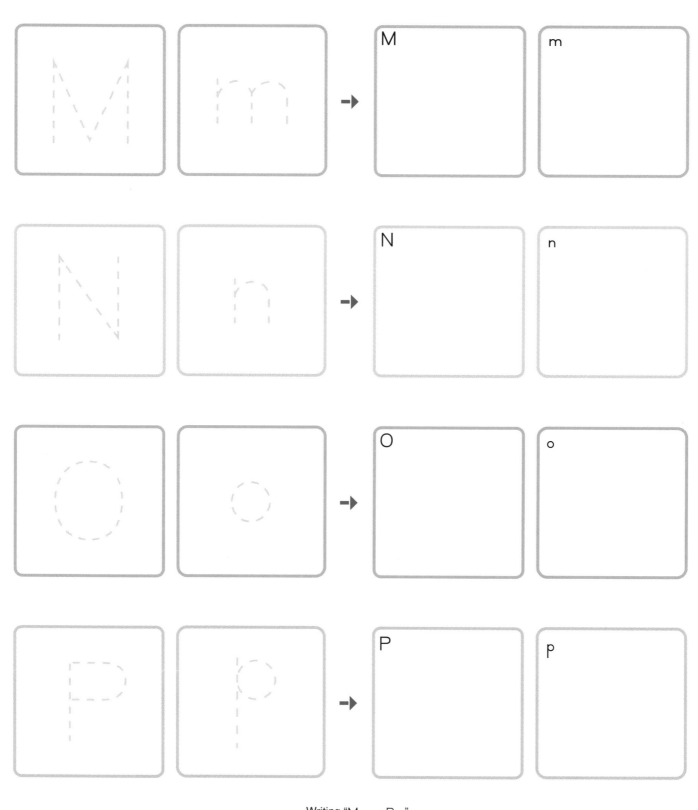

Upper- and Lower-case Letters
Writing "Q·q/R·r"

Name

Date

■ Look at the first letters of the words below. Then trace the letters.

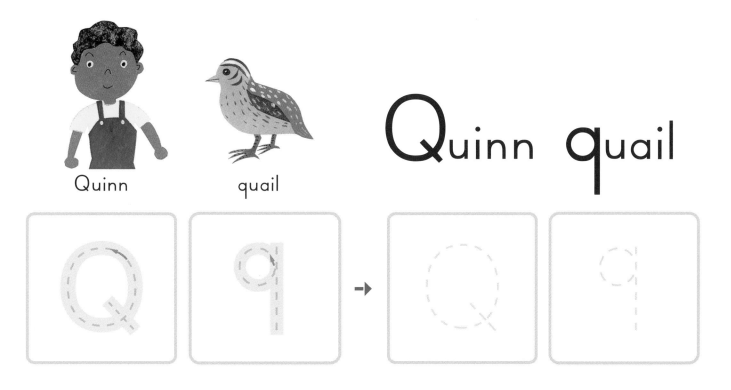

Quinn   quail

Quinn   quail

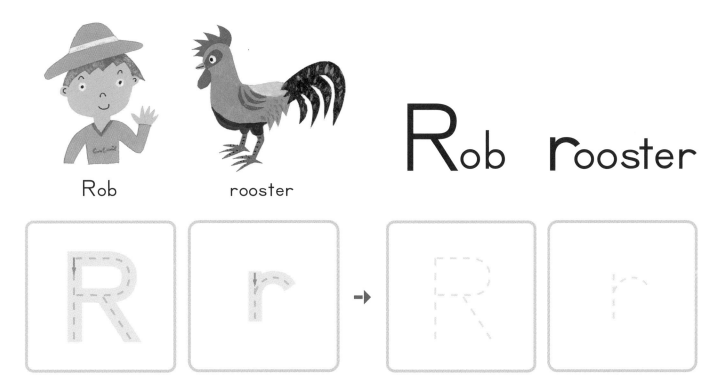

Rob   rooster

Rob   rooster

Writing "Q·q / R·r"

■ Trace and then write each letter while saying it aloud.

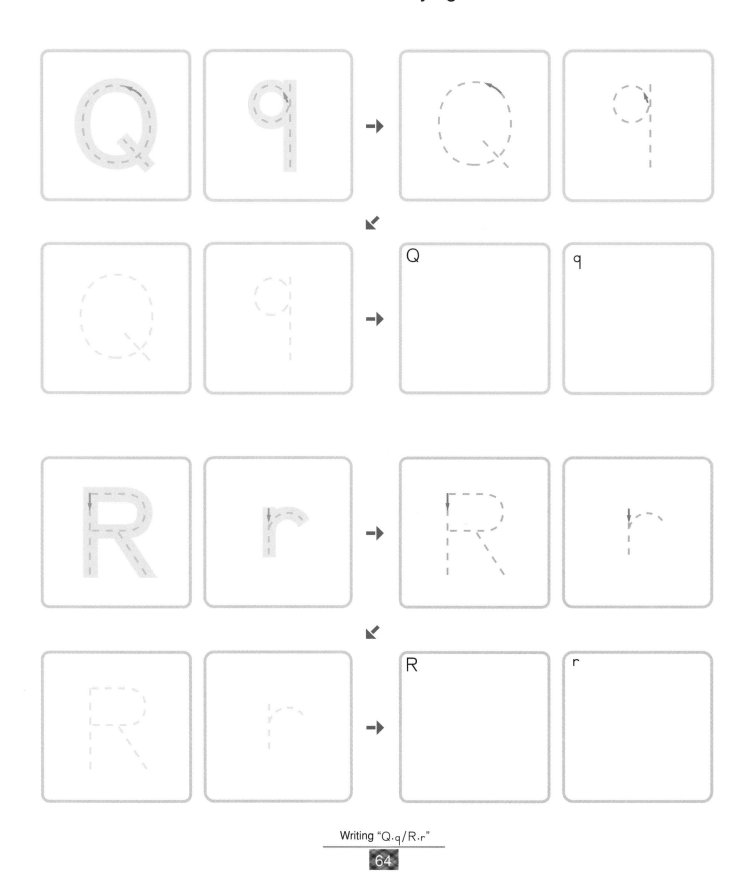

33

Upper- and Lower-case Letters
Writing "S·s / T·t"

Name

Date

■ Look at the first letters of the words below. Then trace the letters.

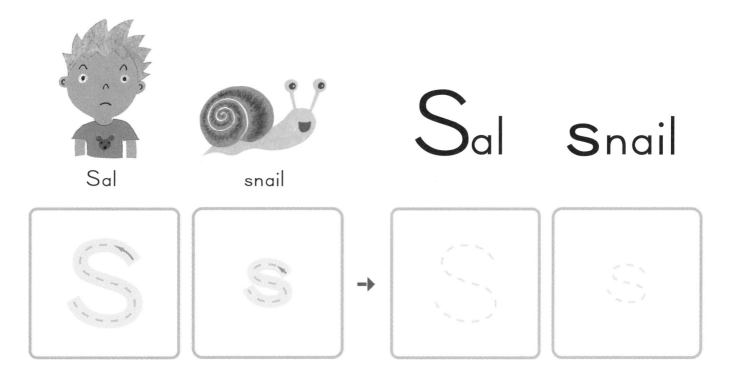

Sal   snail   Sal   Snail

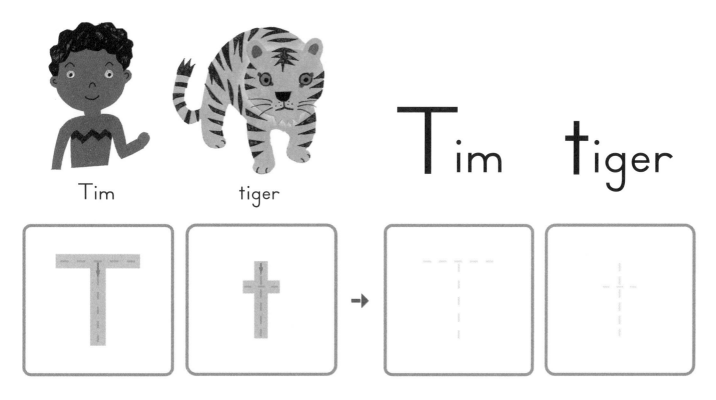

Tim   tiger   Tim   tiger

Writing "S.s / T.t"

■ Trace and then write each letter while saying it aloud.

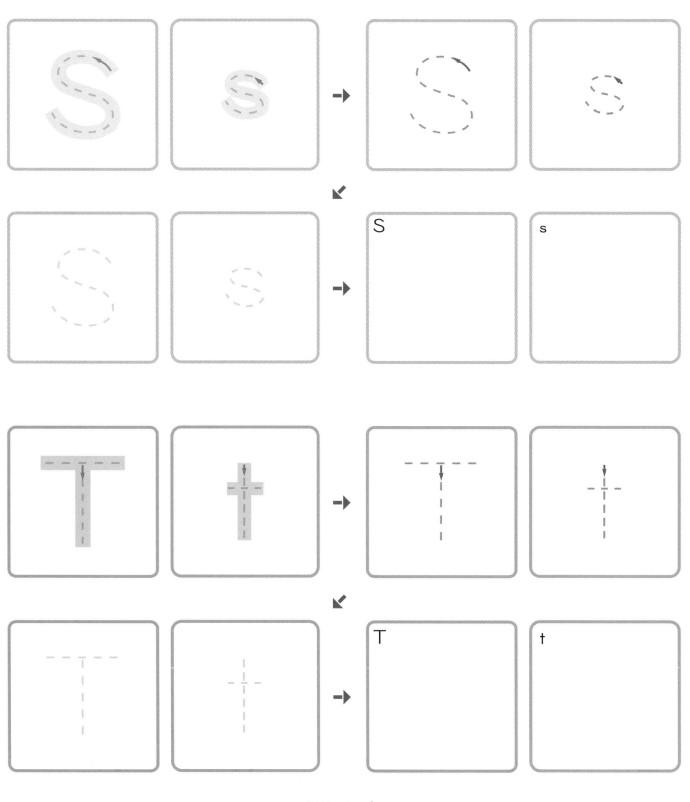

Review

Writing "Q·q→ T·t"

Name
Date

■ Trace each letter while saying it aloud.

  →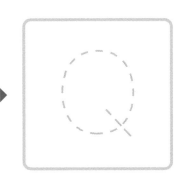

  →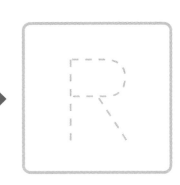

  →

  →

Writing "Q·q→T·t"

■ Trace and then write each letter while saying it aloud.

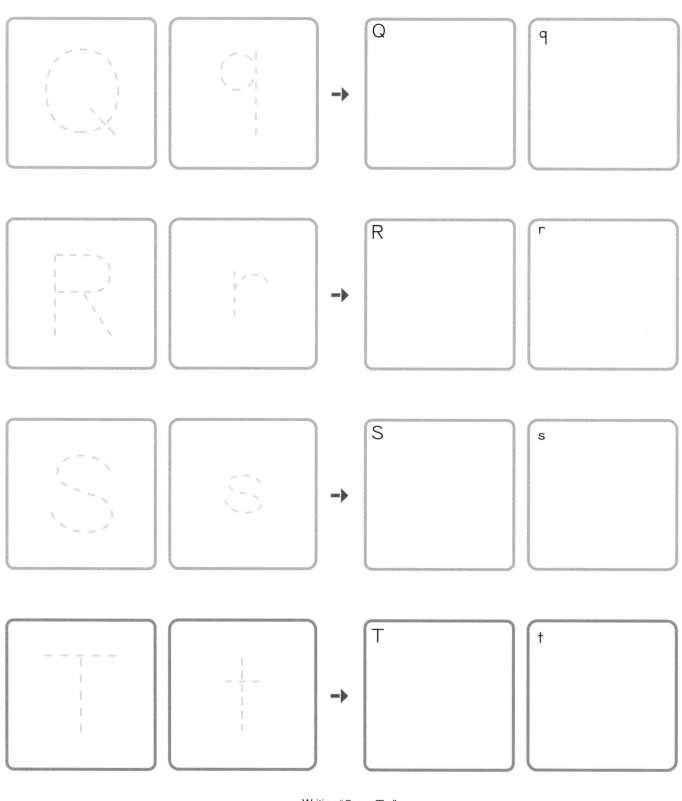

35

Upper- and Lower-case Letters

Writing "U·u / V·v"

Name

Date

■ Look at the first letters of the words below. Then trace the letters.

Uma   unicorn

Uma Unicorn

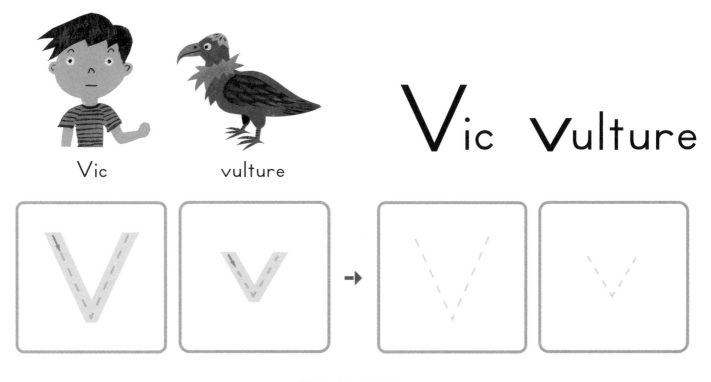

Vic   vulture

Vic Vulture

Writing "U·u / V·v"

■ Trace and then write each letter while saying it aloud.

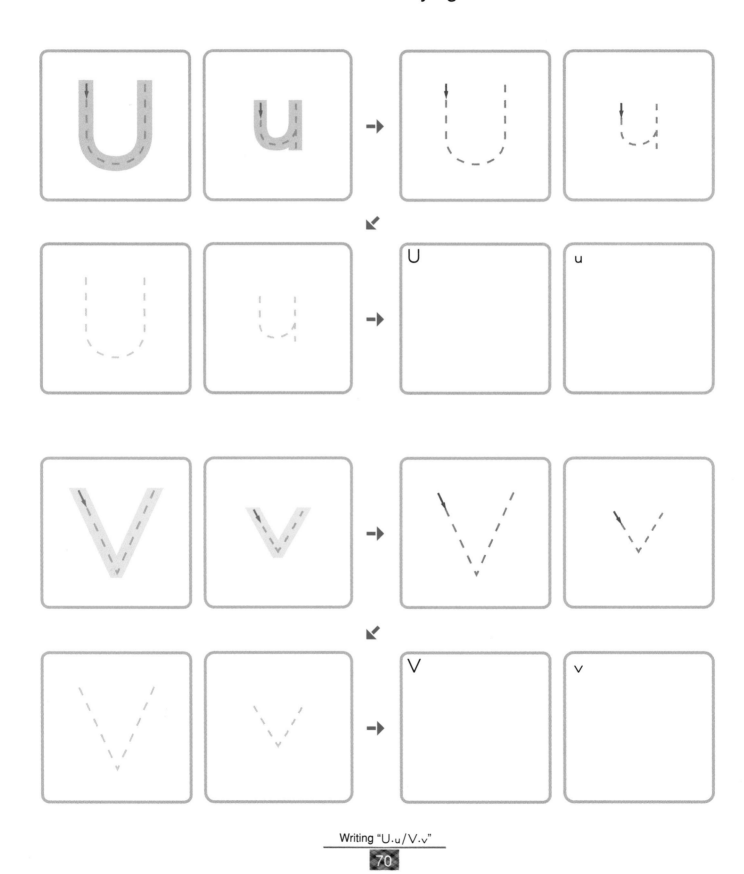

36

Upper- and Lower-case Letters
Writing "W·w/X·x"

Name

Date

■ Look at the first letters of the words below. Then trace the letters.

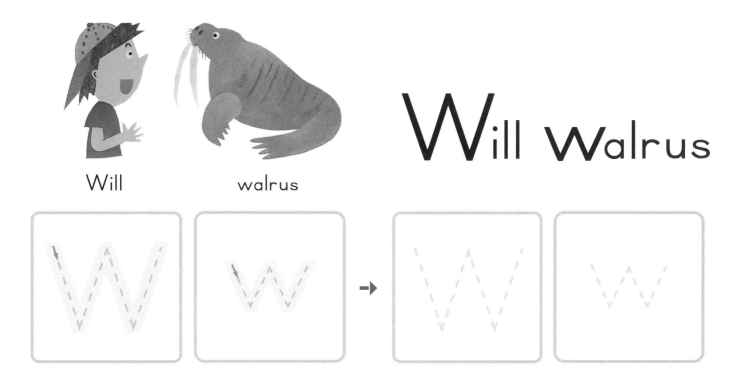

Will   walrus

Will Walrus

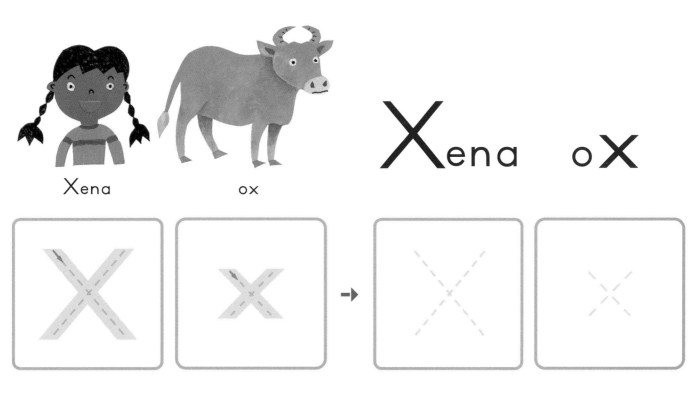

Xena   ox

Xena   oX

Writing "W.w/X.x"

■ Trace and then write each letter while saying it aloud.

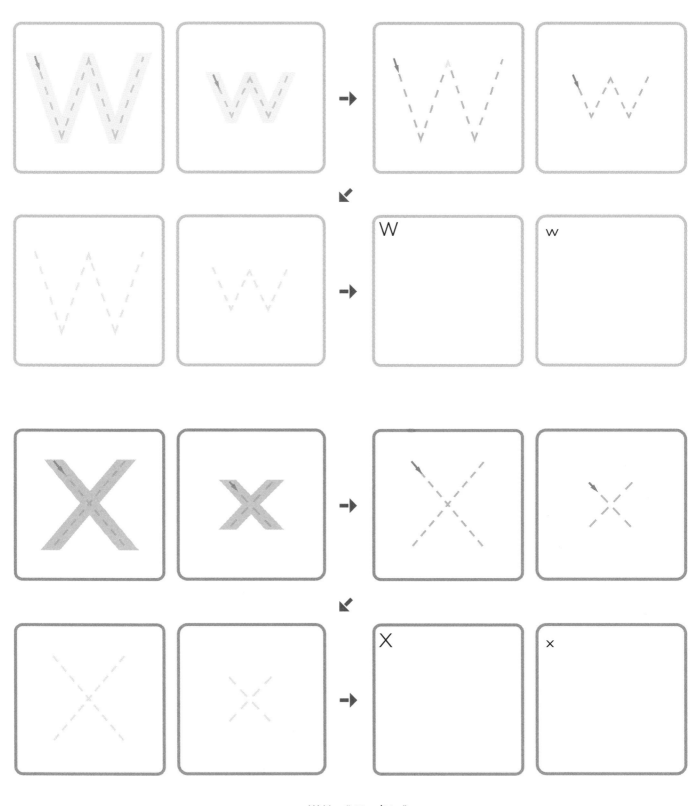

37 Review
Writing "U·u → X·x"

Name

Date

■ Trace each letter while saying it aloud.

Writing "U·u → X·x"

■ Trace and then write each letter while saying it aloud.

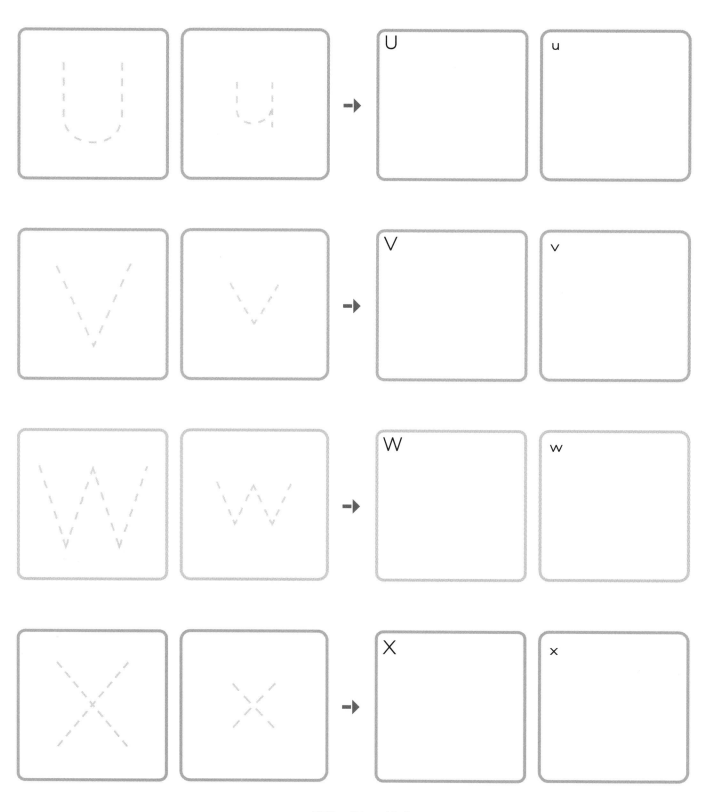

Upper- and Lower-case Letters
Writing "Y·y/Z·z"

Name

Date

■ Look at the first letters of the words below. Then trace the letters.

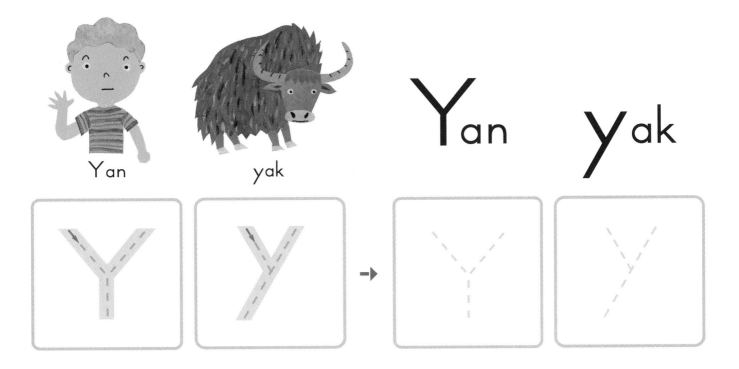

Yan

yak

Yan   Yak

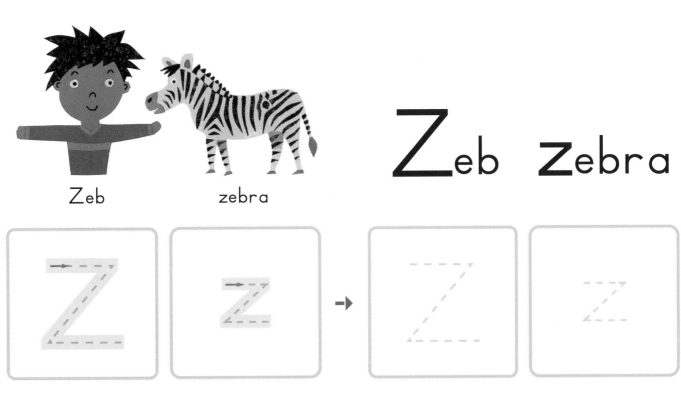

Zeb   zebra

Zeb   Zebra

Writing "Y·y / Z·z"

■ Trace and then write each letter while saying it aloud.

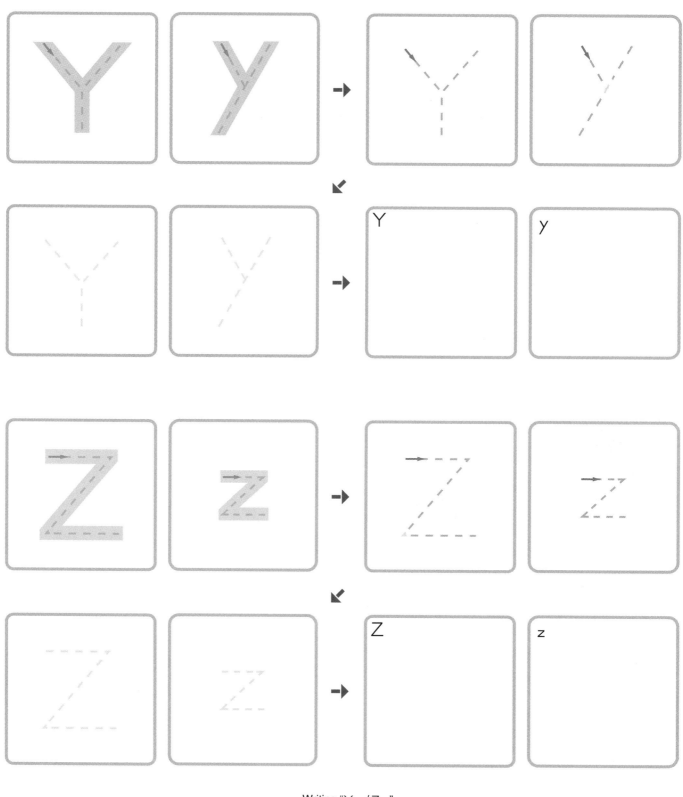

Review

Writing "Y·y → Z·z"

Name
Date

■ Trace each letter while saying it aloud.

Y y → Y Y

Z z → Z Z

Y Y → Y y

Z Z → Z z

Writing "A·a → I·i"

■ Write each letter while saying it aloud.

A	a	B	b
C	c	D	d
E	e	F	f
G	g	H	h
I	i		

Review
Writing "J・j→R・r"

■ Write each letter while saying it aloud.

J	j	K	k
L	l	M	m
N	n	O	o
P	p	Q	q
R	r		

Writing "S·s ➔ Z·z"

■ Write each letter while saying it aloud.

S	s	T	t
U	u	V	v
W	w	X	x
Y	y	Z	z